# IAN HORROCKS
# Newcastle United
## A PHOTOGRAPHIC HISTORY OF A MOMENTOUS DECADE

The **Hallamshire** Press 2000

All photographs by Ian Horrocks
Photographs © 2000 Newcastle United Football Club,
Ian Horrocks and the Newcastle Evening Chronicle
Text © 2000 The Hallamshire Press

**Published by The Hallamshire Press Limited**
**Broom Hall**
**Sheffield S10 2DR**
**UK**

Typeset and designed by The Hallamshire Press Limited
Printed in Singapore

British Library Cataloguing in Publication Data:
   A catalogue record for this book is available from the British Library.

ISBN 1 874718 49 0

# Contents

*To Lisa, Jake and Tom*
*for all the late nights and lost weekends*

# Foreword

*Capturing on film the amazing story of Newcastle United in the Nineties was a major task and it took a special sort of photographer to accomplish it.*

*Ian Horrocks is that special sort of photographer—as good a 'snapper' as there is, and the set of pictures in this book tell a remarkable story in excellent style.*

*I was fortunate to be a part of the Newcastle United success story of the Nineties. Having left the club in 1987 for Liverpool, I returned at the age of 32 in 1993 and I can honestly say that second four-year spell was my most exciting in football—bar none.*

*The team Kevin Keegan put together, with David Ginola, Les Ferdinand, Alan Shearer and all the rest, was the most exciting I ever played in. And that included the great Liverpool side of the late Eighties.*

*The Nineties was a decade that began with struggle and became a phenomenon; Ian saw it all and photographed it all, home and abroad, built up a veritable treasure-trove of photographs, and I'm delighted to see justice done to them in this fascinating book.*

*Ian doesn't only cover matches. He has a smashing personality, and he's become a friend of the players, too. He does jobs for the lads away from the game, including myself, and he was kind enough to produce a special portfolio on my testimonial in 1999 which is a wonderful keepsake for myself, my wife Sandra, and our children Drew and Stacey.*

*The reconstruction of St James' Park has also kept Ian busy clambering around on ladders and rooftops for yet more vantage points and new pictures. The chapter on the stadium, bringing the rebuilding right up to date, is especially interesting.*

*As a Geordie lad, I'm delighted to see the new St James' Park looking so good. But I'm also proud and delighted at what I see as a vital factor—the club hasn't moved out. Sunderland and Middlesbrough switched to new grounds in the Nineties, but happily Newcastle United are still at their spiritual home, and for Geordies like me that's very important.*

*Mind you, St James' looks a bit different from the old days, when you could see the floodlights from miles around. Those tall pylons were the landmarks then— now the massive stands are the landmarks, and a truly glorious sight they make from all approaches to the city.*

*With a 52,000 capacity and the right man leading the team in Bobby Robson, I'm sure there will in the years ahead be many more special Newcastle United moments demanding special photographs. And that's where Ian Horrocks comes in.*

Peter Beardsley MBE

# Introduction

Perhaps no-one gets a better close-up view than a photographer, and Ian Horrocks has been as close as anyone to the remarkable story of Newcastle United in the Nineties.

Even before joining United as official club photographer in September 1994, Ian frequently covered matches while working for the Newcastle Chronicle and Journal.

But as the club photographer, travelling everywhere with the team, covering events off and on the field, and seeing every minute of every game, Ian has been an integral part of the Newcastle United scene for the past six years.

When Alan Shearer signed for £15m in 1996, Ian travelled with him to the Far East to join his team-mates on tour.

And when United faced the cream of Europe, destroyed Manchester United 5–0, and reached two successive FA Cup Finals, Ian was there every step of the way.

The exclusive access to Newcastle United he has enjoyed means no-one is better placed to produce an intimate photographic record of the era.

This book is the result.

'There have been many, many highs as well as one or two lows with Newcastle United in the Nineties,' Ian says, 'but the beauty of it all has been that the managers and players I've worked with have all been tremendously friendly and helpful.

'I've formed a good relationship with them all and enjoyed the job—but it's better than a job, really.'

Born and bred in Winlaton, south of the Tyne, Ian joined the Gateshead Post in 1982 as a 16-year-old darkroom printer and studied photo-journalism at Stradbroke College, Sheffield, in 1984.

In 1986 he joined the Stewart Bonney Agency in Newcastle, working for national newspapers, and had a second spell with Bonney between two spells with the Newcastle Chronicle and Journal.

In 1990, Ian won the North-East Sports Council Picture of the Year award for a shot taken at the Great North Run, and in 1996 the trip to the Far East with Alan Shearer paid dividends when one close-up shot won him the Media Sports Photo of the Year award.

Married to Lisa—'she's also a football fan'—Ian is the father of two boys, ten-year-old Jake, who plays in goal for his local junior side, and six-year-old Tom.

Of all the great games Ian has covered as Newcastle United photographer, his own personal favourite is the 5–0 slaughter of champions Manchester United at St James' Park in October 1996.

'After losing the title to them so heartbreakingly in 1995–96, and then losing 4–0 to them in the Charity Shield at Wembley, we went into that match looking for a bit of revenge—maybe a narrow 1–0 victory,' he recalls.

'But on the day, everything clicked into place, the lads produced the best team performance I've seen in all my time with Newcastle United, and the whole occasion was as perfect as it could be. Manchester United got off lightly with 5–0.

'A lot of people prefer the 3–2 Champions League victory over Barcelona in '97, but they remember that as much for Tino Asprilla's hat-trick as anything; the TEAM performance against Manchester United was the thing which elevated it above Barcelona in my mind.

'Disappointments? Well, losing two successive FA Cup Finals in 1998 and 1999 was hard to take.

'But you learn to take the rough with the smooth in this game.'

Ian Horrocks

# The managers

Jim Smith began the Nineties in charge of Newcastle but he described United as 'unmanageable' in the midst of the Magpie Group takeover saga and left in 1991. Smith was replaced by former Argentinian international Ossie Ardiles, but the team's fortunes continued to slide. After a disastrous 5–2 defeat at Oxford United, the taciturn Ardiles merely shrugged when asked by the directors if he could save United from relegation to Division Three. Within four days, early on the morning of February 5th, 1992, Ardiles was informed of his dismissal and held an impromptu press conference at his city centre home.

On the same day that Ardiles was sacked, the Messiah came home. Kevin Keegan, having spent eight years at leisure in Spain, was persuaded to return to St James' Park on a short-term agreement with one target: to save Newcastle United from the dreaded drop.

When, in May 1984, Kevin Keegan retired as a player with mission accomplished and Newcastle United promoted to Division One, no-one ever dared guess he would return as manager just eight years later. The Messianic effect of Keegan on United between 1982 and 1984 can never be underestimated, and the emotional farewell he received from the United fans after his final match in the 3–1 victory over Brighton reflected the adoration of the masses for him. The now-famous Brighton game, described by Peter Beardsley as 'pure theatre' was, as it turned out, a mere adieu for Keegan.

Kevin Keegan may be taking the micky out of Terry McDermott's curly-perm haircut, but Keegan valued his 'buffer' highly. McDermott, a playing colleague of Keegan's at Newcastle and Liverpool, took much of the pressure and many of the tasks of management off Keegan's hands.

Keegan, as he had been between 1982 and 1984, was a phenomenon in every way. Unrivalled as a PR man, he frequently found time to meet the people of Tyneside who idolised him, and here he is pictured with workers at the Swan Hunter shipyard in Wallsend.

The 1992–93 season, in which United took the First Division Championship with a breathtaking brand of swashbuckling attacking football, was the birth of the Newcastle United miracle. After the season's final match, a dazzling 7–1 home victory over Leicester City, Keegan led his side on an unforgettable lap of honour which drew the sort of ovation not heard at St James' for many a long year.

KK's grey hair was still to come, but in the summer of 1996 he was made up to appear aged alongside the eternally youthful Peter Beardsley as part of a promotional campaign for United's kit suppliers, Adidas.

In January 1995, to the dismay of United fans everywhere, Keegan sold leading scorer Andy Cole, the man he had brought to Tyneside two years earlier from Bristol City, to title rivals Manchester United. As the sensational news spread, baffled supporters gathered at the main entrance to St James' Park—and Keegan himself emerged to explain his reasons. 'There's a bullet with my name on it if I've got it wrong', he said later. But he hadn't got it wrong, and signed Les Ferdinand the following summer.

The European Championships came to Newcastle in the summer of 1996, and Kevin, ever the public relations star, gave this little girl a helping hand, as well as an arm and a foot, in a kiddies' dribbling skills competition.

Kevin led a party of youngsters on a United-organised trip to Lapland to meet the 'real' Santa Claus. It was Christmas 1996 and one lucky youngster got his present-of-a-lifetime as the United boss gave him a backriding sledge run. Despite frost on his eyebrows, KK was still able to deliver a warm smile. But the smile would not be there much longer…

Although the damage to him of the second-place finish to Manchester United in 1995–96 never truly healed, Keegan nonetheless led United back into Europe. Here, in a sleet-soaked training session on the eve of the UEFA Cup third round tie in France against Metz, Keegan shows signs of the tension beginning to envelop him.

All good things come to an end, and when the clouds started to gather over the Kevin Keegan reign at Christmas 1996, the Messiah's departure was only weeks away. Despite a 7–1 destruction of Tottenham and a 3–0 demolition of Leeds, Keegan was gone by January 8th, 1997. The pictures of a pensive and unhappy Keegan, his chin buried in a raised collar, are burned into the psyche of every Newcastle supporter.

When Keegan finally broke his ties with United in January 1997, after a 1–1 FA Cup third round draw at Charlton, the United Board moved quickly to recruit a replacement. Bobby Robson, then at Barcelona, was approached, but when Robson elected to remain loyal to the Spanish giants, United instead installed former Liverpool and Blackburn manager Kenny Dalglish as Keegan's replacement. Dalglish, his reputation at a high following title glory with Blackburn, was mobbed by the fans upon his arrival on Tyneside on January 14th, 1997.

Barely 24 hours later, Dalglish watched his new charges for the first time in a difficult Cup replay with Charlton. Terry McDermott, Keegan's sidekick since 1992 and a former playing colleague of Dalglish at Liverpool, stayed to work with the Scotsman and came out on the pitch with him before the Charlton replay to take the ovation of the supporters. United beat the Londoners 2–1 in extra time and the Dalglish show was on the road.

At the age of 45, like Keegan, Dalglish was a tracksuit manager who liked nothing better than getting out on the training ground with the players to whom he remained intensely loyal, even in the face of public criticism.

Although King Kenny's FA Cup hopes in 1997 were ended by a shock Nottingham Forest victory at St James' Park in the fourth round just 12 days after the Scot's arrival, he still piloted the side through a League run of only two defeats in 15 games before the final match of the season, ironically, at home to Nottingham Forest. United's 5–0 slaughter of Forest, combined with Liverpool's failure to win at Sheffield Wednesday, meant the Magpies again finished second—but this time, under new qualification rules, that meant a place in the UEFA Champions' Cup.

Manager with a mission: Kenny Dalglish leads out his Newcastle team for the 1998 FA Cup Final against Arsenal, holding the hand of a young fan suffering from a serious heart complaint who was chosen to walk out with the players at Wembley. The day ended with United surrendering weakly, 2–0, and the United fans at the Tunnel End imploring their side to 'Attack, Attack, Attack'.

Two games into the 1998–99 season,
Dalglish and United parted
company amid bitter counter-
recriminations. With Dalglish gone,
the rumour factory went into
overtime, and local radio station
Metro FM made the most of it with a
series of spoof placards
foreshadowing prospective new
managers. Ruud Gullit may not
have been seen in the Bigg Market
before Dalglish's departure, but he
was certainly seen in the city very
soon thereafter.

Charismatic, proud and
dreadlocked, Dutchman Gullit
replaced Dalglish just before the
third game of the 1998–99 season—
and beguiled the national and
international press on the day of his
appointment with the multi-lingual
eloquence for which he had become
famous at Chelsea.

The arrival of Ruud Gullit sparked
a new wave of interest—and a new
wave of business for the club shop.
Leisure-wear bearing the
Dutchman's name fills the window
while the fans gather outside.

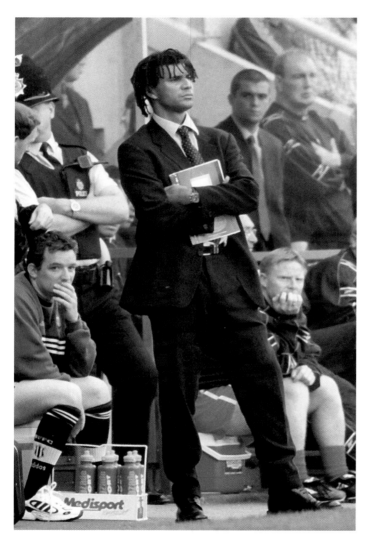

In his first match, Gullit looked on in despair as a horribly-disorganised side was trampled underfoot by Liverpool, who went away from Tyneside with a 4–1 victory and a Michael Owen hat-trick. Gullit knew instantly his job was going to be hard, and said: 'It is very difficult to make everything work immediately. But it was all very interesting to see.'

Gullit's quality as a player with some of the world's greatest teams had never been in doubt, and when he donned the black-and-white stripes for a pre-season friendly at Reading on July 24th, 1999, much of that quality was still in evidence. With his side 2–0 down at half-time, the Dutchman came off the substitutes' bench to inspire a fightback to 2–2 and spark calls for a return to playing which he immediately rejected. He would not be around much longer to play for—or manage—Newcastle United.

The 'rain' is nearly over…rain-soaked Ruud Gullit stands forlornly on the touchline as his Sunderland counterpart Peter Reid animatedly issues instructions during United's cataclysmic 2–1 defeat in the August 1999 derby at St James' Park. The symbolic deluge brought about the end to the Gullit reign. Three days later he announced his resignation.

On September 3rd, 1999, Bobby Robson, 66, was unveiled as the new manager of Newcastle United. For the man from Langley Park, Co Durham, it was a poignant homecoming to the club he loves best after half a century in the game which had taken him around Europe. Two-and-a-half years earlier, upon Kevin Keegan's departure, Robson had been approached but remained loyal to Barcelona. Now the way was clear for Bobby's Job. And his impact on Newcastle United was both positive and immediate.

The England club: past England team managers Bobby Robson and Graham Taylor share a joke with Alan Shearer before the match at Watford in November 1999.

If looks could kill…Robson takes exception to a linesman's offside decision in the return game with Watford in March 2000.

Many eyebrows were raised at United's appointment of a 66-year-old manager, but Bobby Robson quickly proved the truth of the old saying that you're only as old as you feel. The tracksuit belongs to Robson every bit as much as Kevin Keegan, Kenny Dalglish or Ruud Gullit.

# The players

NEWCASTLE UNITED

One of the most important factors in the transition from also-rans to Football League title winners, Gavin Peacock, signed from Bournemouth in a part-exchange deal in November 1990, produced compelling displays, scoring 47 goals in 120 appearances from midfield before joining Chelsea in the summer of 1993.

Micky Quinn was the goalscoring hero who scored four times on his United debut in 1989 and carried the main goal threat through the difficult early Nineties, averaging more than a goal every two games. But the quality of new arrivals like Andy Cole squeezed him out of the first-team picture.

Described by Kevin Keegan as one of the most important figures in the history of Newcastle United, rugged centre-back Brian Kilcline shored up an ailing side and in his two years on Tyneside, helped lay the foundations for future prosperity. A crucial element in the 1992–93 survival battle, 'Killer' arrived from Oldham for £250,000 in early 1992 and, job done, moved on to Swindon for £90,000 in January 1994.

Has any Newcastle player ever scored a more important goal than David Kelly's 85th-minute winner against Portsmouth in the penultimate game of the 1991–92 season? His brilliant half-volley at the Gallowgate End gave United a lifeline to cling onto—and a week later, victory at Leicester sealed the great escape from demotion to Division Three. Kelly, an intelligent, old-fashioned inside-forward, showed great skill and inventiveness but was sold by Kevin Keegan in June 1993. When the Premier League glory days came along, Kelly was never forgotten by the fans who owed him so much.

*All aboard for the big drive through the Premier League! Kevin Keegan and Terry McDermott get the wheels in motion, with stars like Barry Venison, Andy Cole and Philippe Albert joining Geordie boys Robbie Elliott, Peter Beardsley, Lee Clark and Steve Watson.*

The £250,000 signing of full-back Barry Venison from Liverpool was a Kevin Keegan masterstroke. Consett-born Venison added great experience to the defence in the side which stormed to the First Division Championship and so high in the Premier League that, well…he needed this oxygen tank to get used to the height.

Belgian central defender Philippe Albert celebrates his first goal for Newcastle, in a Coca-Cola Cup victory over Manchester United at St James' Park in October 1994. Albert, known as 'Prince' in his own country, became one of the most cultured players in Britain following his £2.65m transfer from Anderlecht on the eve of the 1994–95 season.

As part of the shock deal of 1995 which took Andy Cole to Manchester United, Irish winger Keith Gillespie came the other way. One of the young stars who matured alongside players like David Beckham and Paul Scholes at Old Trafford, Gillespie suffered a couple of serious injuries and never quite hit the jackpot at Newcastle.

One of Sir John Hall's declared ambitions was to have a team of Geordies at Newcastle United, and none was more Geordie at heart than Wallsend lad Lee Clark. An English international midfielder at Schools, Youth and Under-21 levels, Clark was Player of the Year and ever-present in United's 1992–93 First Division Championship season. However, unable to hold down a regular first-team place in the top flight, he left St James' Park for, of all places, Sunderland, in 1997, and later joined Fulham…under Kevin Keegan.

One of the many successful branches of Newcastle United has been the Junior Magpies Club, and the United players frequently attend club functions. Barry Venison finds his hands full dealing with one rather young fan at a signing session.

Another of the Geordie contingent, left-back Robbie Elliott understudied John Beresford for long periods but never let the side down when called upon. When Gosforth-born Elliott and North Shields-born Steve Watson occupied the full-back positions in a match at West Ham in April 1991, the two Geordies set a new record for the youngest full-back pairing in United's history.

In two four-year spells with Newcastle United, Peter Beardsley surpassed all superlatives and laid arguable claim to the honour of being the club's greatest-ever player. Plucked from the obscurity of American football by Arthur Cox in 1983, Beardsley teamed up with Kevin Keegan and Chris Waddle to give the side the extra push needed for promotion to Division One.

When, after six years on Merseyside with Liverpool and Everton, Beardsley returned to Tyneside for £1.5m in July 1993, many experts said he was too old at 32. But he confounded the critics with another four years of brilliance, and the MBE he was awarded in 1995 for services to football was thoroughly deserved. Wife Sandra and children Drew and Stacey help him display the MBE outside Buckingham Palace.

When Keegan sold Andy Cole to Manchester United in January 1995, and the season faded away into failure, many a question was asked. But when Keegan paid Queen's Park Rangers £6m for England leader Les Ferdinand, another big name was added to the gallery of great Number Nines to have played for United. In two years, the man the fans dubbed 'Sir Les' scored 50 goals and in 1996–97 formed an awesome front-line partnership with Alan Shearer. His sale to Tottenham in the summer of 1997 caused major controversy.

*Destined to be ever popular with the Geordies, Les Ferdinand is greeted by a mass of cheering fans on the day he joins United, and signs the first of countless autographs.*

*Perhaps more than any other player, Frenchman David Ginola came to personify the extravagant brilliance of Newcastle United in the mid-1990s. Stylish, swaggering and supremely skilful, the man with the film star face captivated the United fans…as well as the Press, to whom he talks at the foot of the stand on the day he signed in July 1995.*

*We did get our hands on the Championship trophy…but sadly, this was BEFORE the 1995–96 season, rather than after it. It belonged to Manchester United by May 1996.*

One of the tallest players ever to sign for Newcastle was goalkeeper Shaka Hislop, a 6ft 4in goalkeeper recruited by Kevin Keegan from Reading in August 1995. Chief Executive Freddie Fletcher enlists the help of a stepladder to get a Size 11 handshake from Hislop, who was born in London of Caribbean parents, and whose name originates from that of a Zulu king.

The summer of 1995 was marked by a frenzy of transfer activity, and when £4m full-back Warren Barton arrived from Wimbledon the media again descended on St James' for interviews…with both manager and new buy.

Newcastle United footballers enjoy the status of gods on Tyneside, and a visit to youngsters in hospital can do more than medicine to speed a cure. Here, Peter Beardsley brings a smile to the face of a youngster in traction.

Stars of pitch and screen, Les Ferdinand and Peter Beardsley label themselves for The Big Breakfast TV show.

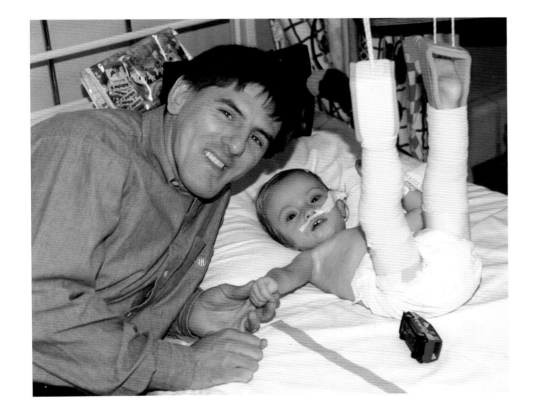

For as long as sand, sea and
Newcastle United have existed, the
club's players have used the bracing
sea air and beaches for occasional
training stints. The class of '96
sprints along Tynemouth Sands on a
cold January day with Steve Watson
and Robbie Elliott leading the field.

The Italian job: In his pursuit of the
best in football, Sir John Hall sent a
three-man delegation to Italy to
produce a report on Lazio's training
facilities. A certain Mr Gascoigne
welcomes United's youth development supremo Chris McMenemy,
physio Paul Ferris, and player Scott
Sellars.

New goalkeeper Shaka Hislop
signed a big boot deal with Adidas
in the summer of 1996. And BIG
was the operative word. For Shaka's
Size 11s filled the biggest and the
best of boots. Kevin Keegan, with a
little help from a box, offers support.

Warming up for the 1995–96 season, United's first-team squad spills sweat on a gruelling training run in the summer sun.

Philippe Albert, Steve Watson, Darren Peacock, Warren Barton and Robbie Elliott set the pace.

Les Ferdinand became another Newcastle star to sign a major boot sponsorship deal with Adidas, and here Les puts his left foot forward to illustrate the fact.

In front of a backdrop announcing the name, the world's most expensive footballer, Alan Shearer, talks to the Press and invited guests at the lavish signing ceremony following his £15m move from Blackburn Rovers in 1996....

...and outside St James' Park, Geordie-boy-come-home Shearer acknowledges the cheers of the thousands of supporters who packed the Castle Leazes car park to welcome him back to Tyneside. The bond between the fans and Shearer, as one of their own, has always been strong.

Dedicated followers of fashion: recruited as models for a 1996 fashion show at St James' Park, Shaka Hislop, Warren Barton, David Ginola and Les Ferdinand prepare to strut their stuff on the catwalk.

England midfield ball-winner David Batty shows off his medals and caps after signing for United from Blackburn in February 1996. It seemed 'Batts' was joining a Championship-bound side…but on his debut, Manchester United snatched a crucial 1–0 victory at St James' Park and went on to overhaul Newcastle in the race for the Premier League title.

East End boy Lee Clark was always one of the dressing-room jokers in his eight years with Newcastle, and here he seems to be rehearsing something between an Al Jolson act and a goalkeeper's stance.

The dreaded white shirt—awarded to the day's worst trainer—didn't often find its way onto Alan Shearer's back. But in this instance, the United and England striker has to grin and wear it!

Have boots, will travel: As United's popularity soared, kit suppliers Adidas took every opportunity to attach themselves to the phenomenon. Flying Irish winger Keith Gillespie was another player to agree a lucrative deal to wear Adidas' modern, state-of-the-art Predator boots.

All the best, from two of the best…Alan Shearer shares a drink with Newcastle Falcons rugby superstar Inge Tuigamala in their roles as the respective sports' most expensive players. Sir John Hall gave major backing to the development of the city's rugby side under the umbrella of the Sporting Club he saw as a pot of gold at the end of the rainbow.

They hardly know what snow is in Colombia, or even in Italy, but when Colombian international Faustino Asprilla arrived in Newcastle in February 1996 to sign in a sensational £7.5m deal from Parma, the worst of English weather arrived with him. But the snowstorm didn't stop the fans, as ever, turning out in force to greet him. Tino, as he became popularly known, was something of an enigma, capable of brilliance and remembered forever for a Champions' League hat-trick against Barcelona; but also capable of frustrating inadequacy.

Pavel Srnicek became one of the most popular players ever to turn out for Newcastle in the years after being signed by Jim Smith for a mere £350,000 in 1990–91. The giant Czech goalkeeper, pictured here at home with wife Pavla and daughter Vendy, struggled at first to adapt to the English game, but persevered and played a major role in the 1992–93 promotion season. The fans' chant of 'Pavel is a Geordie' went to the heart of the gentle giant, who then sported a T-shirt carrying exactly the same message!

Left-back John Beresford could certainly motor…up and down the touchline and along the dual carriageways. 'Bes', a £650,000 recruit from Portsmouth in the summer of 1992, was part of the United success story for over five years before moving to Southampton. Off the field, 'Bes' was a sports car fanatic—and much of those many win bonuses he earned at Newcastle went on a glittering collection of MGs, some of which he proudly displays here.

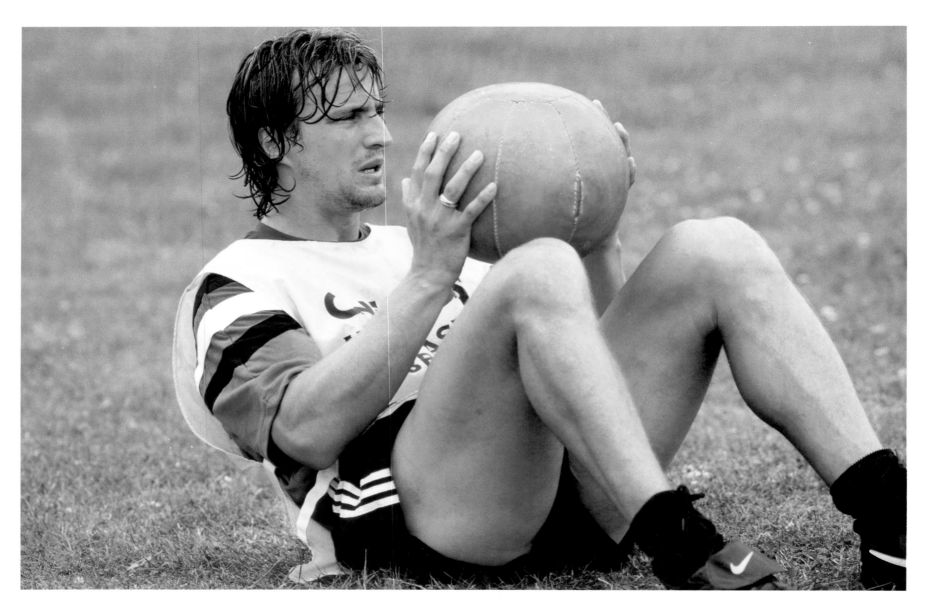

*Proof that David Ginola did occasionally break sweat. The bedraggled look certainly wasn't part of his image, and the medicine ball wasn't his favourite tool of the trade. Who'd have thought this man would be advertising shampoo in later years?*

*Veterans on parade: Stuart Pearce and Ian Rush were both into their mid-30s when they signed for Newcastle under Kenny Dalglish. Pearce, caught on camera making a friendly gesture towards the photographer, played a significant role, not least in the 1997–98 Champions League campaign, but former Liverpool star Rush failed to make a major impact, scoring only twice in 14 appearances.*

Steve Watson was one of the Geordie lads around whom a dream was built. Along with Lee Clark and Robbie Elliott, Steve came through the junior ranks to make a big name for himself as a versatile, play-anywhere star. Ironically, his very versatility threatened to deny him a regular place, and even when he settled down at right-back, he didn't keep the spot, and was eventually sold for £4m to Aston Villa in October 1998.

A different kind of club, a different kind of ball…but golf is a shared passion among the majority of footballers, and a pre-season trip to Dublin in 1998 gives Gary Speed, Rob Lee and Alan Shearer a chance to perfect the putting technique. Looks as though Gary still has a little work to do, though, as his ball skids past the hole.

The Peacock's tail: Centre-half Darren Peacock arrived from Queen's Park Rangers in March 1994 with long, flowing hair; the only concession he made was to pack it into a ponytail. Tall and fearless, Peacock formed excellent centre-back partnerships with both Philippe Albert and Steve Howey and played 175 times for United before joining Blackburn Rovers in the 1998 close season.

Two of Colombian Tino Asprilla's great passions were horses and horseracing, and this mount, kept at stables in Lanchester, Co Durham, was named after him. Asprilla—the human being, that is—frequently visited the stables to discuss progress with stable owner Brian Ellison.

Numerous overseas players came to Newcastle United during the Nineties, and most spoke decent English, but Italian defender Alessandro Pistone knew little of the lingo and was swiftly enrolled into English language classes with a specially-hired teacher. Despite the best possible tuition and books, he couldn't find anywhere the Italian equivalent of 'Howay the Lads'.

Chief Cook and…goalkeeper. Among Trinidadian Shaka Hislop's many talents was a propensity for cooking, and he wasn't slow to rustle up some Caribbean specialities for his new team-mates. With a chef's hat atop his 6ft 4in frame, Shaka had trouble getting into the kitchen!

*The one and only Paul Gascoigne started out at Newcastle in the mid-80s—and drama and controversy followed him around. More than that followed Gazza around when he played for Middlesbrough against Newcastle at the Riverside Stadium in December 1998. First, his son Regan followed him onto the pitch as match mascot…then two shapely girl streakers wearing (or not, as the case may be) Santa Claus outfits, pursued him across the pitch. Never a dull moment with Gazza around…*

Andy Cole was a virtual unknown when Kevin Keegan plucked him from the obscurity of Bristol City for £1.75m to put the finishing touches to the 1992–93 promotion campaign. Cole went on to become one of the principal figures in United's rapid rise to the top, scoring 68 goals in 84 appearances—including a record-breaking 41 in 45 in 1993–94—before his shock £7m sale to Manchester United in 1995. Lean, lithe and hungry for goals, Cole was an instant hero among heroes and earned his place in the famous Newcastle United No 9 gallery.

Elegant and highly-skilled, Belgian international centre-back Philippe Albert was Kevin Keegan's 'next step' in the building of a superteam when he signed from Anderlecht for £2.65m in August 1994. More than most of the foreign imports, Albert settled happily into the Tyneside way of life with wife Katty and daughter Julie, pictured here with her father at their home in the city.

*Stretch…Greek defender Nikos Dabizas goes to toe-touching extremes in training exercises…*

*…while Georgian Temuri Ketsbaia takes an upside-down look at the world. Dabizas and Ketsbaia were part of a massive influx of foreign players at a time when the English transfer market almost priced itself outside the bounds of reality.*

*Paintball Private Alan Shearer poses in Army fatigues while physio Derek Wright shows the wounds of war. Wimbledon away? No—this was manager Ruud Gullit's scheme to build team spirit: paintballing in woods near Slaley in the Tyne Valley. The players and coaches split into teams and, under supervised instruction, fired pot-shots at one another from paint-guns. It gave another meaning to 'Painting The Toon Red'.*

*Rome from home…former United favourite Mick Martin outside the Rome Coliseum during United's UEFA Cup visit to the Eternal City in November 1999. Former Eire international Martin, who played for United between 1978 and 1983, runs a business on Tyneside and operates as expert analyst at United matches for local radio station Metro FM.*

The first Peruvian ever to play in the English League, Nolberto Solano brought not only South American soccer skills to Tyneside, but also South American culture. An expert musician, Nol plays the trumpet and the drums to a background of Peruvian CDs at his home in Newcastle.

Fast asleep or frozen? No…just goalkeeper Shay Given's unusual stretching exercises.

Alan Shearer took six months to get over a ruptured right ankle between July 1997 and February 1998—six months of agony. During the long and arduous rehabilitation course mapped out for him by the United medical staff, Shearer kept the rest of his body in the best possible trim, though doing so with a 'pot' on one leg didn't make it easy.

With the 'pot' off, Shearer walked his way back to happiness… although that smile does look a bit forced.

Veteran North-East scout Jack Hixon was the man who discovered Alan Shearer and hijacked his talents for Southampton in the late 1980s. The two men are now inseparable friends, and appeared with the United idol in the 'My Kinda Town' TV advert for McDonald's.

Making the advert meant getting up at 5.30am on a day off for Alan, and posing on a rainy High Level Bridge. But it all helps sell a lot more McChicken Sandwiches.

Star strikers old and new: Scot Duncan Ferguson arrived from Everton for £8m in November 1998, hit two goals on his debut, and thereafter succumbed to a series of troublesome injuries which severely limited his contribution before his return to Everton in August 2000. But there were clear signs that the Ferguson-Shearer partnership could have been dynamite.

Malcolm Macdonald, one of the all-time United greats, cost a mere £180,000 from Luton Town in 1971; but that was a club record fee at a time when the money in the game was nothing like today. His champagne lifestyle of the time would have been accompanied today by millions in the bank.

*The rain in training…doesn't stop wing wizard David Ginola weaving between some static opponents—but who knocked one down?*

# The games

NEWCASTLE UNITED

Newcastle United began the 1990s in serious decline after losing to Sunderland in the 1989–90 promotion play-offs, and the appointment of Argentinian Ossie Ardiles to replace Jim Smith as manager in 1991 failed to halt the slide. Symbolically, Ardiles' first match, on April Fools' Day 1991, ended in a 2–0 home defeat by Bristol Rovers in front of a meagre 17,509 crowd…

…Ten months later, Ardiles was sacked and replaced by the charismatic Kevin Keegan, who took charge with the team in grave danger of relegation to Division Three. Such was the pulling power of Keegan that 29,263 fans turned up for his first match, a 3–0 home victory over Bristol City.

Although Keegan had an immediate impact on United, a run of five successive defeats left the side on the brink of the drop. A 1–0 home victory over Portsmouth in the season's penultimate match left United needing victory at Leicester on the final day to avoid the trapdoor.

It would prove to be one of the most dramatic and explosive matches in the history of Newcastle United. Gavin Peacock (below) gave United a first-half lead—to the delight of the United bench in the picture on the right.

But when promotion-chasing Leicester equalised through Steve Walsh with only minutes remaining, and the home fans invaded the pitch, the fat was very much in the fire. Several United players later admitted they had no idea whether or not that goal would have sent them down.

It wouldn't have, in fact. But all that became academic when Walsh put through his own goal deep into injury time to give the Magpies a 2–1 victory and guarantee survival …as well as a platform to glory in the rest of the decade.

Perhaps no action photograph of Newcastle United in the 90s means more to the fans than this one. Liam O'Brien curls a wicked free-kick into the Sunderland net in October 1992 to clinch a 2–1 victory. This not only brought United's 11th consecutive league victory but also sealed the first Newcastle triumph at Roker Park for 36 years. The sea of cheering fans behind the Roker End goal rewards close study. It was an early peak in a glorious First Division Championship season, and a moment that will never be forgotten.

On a famous night in humble
Cleethorpes in May 1993, United
finally put the seal on promotion
with a 2–0 victory over Grimsby
Town. Here, Paul Bracewell drives
forward with David Kelly—the
scorer of the second goal—in
support.

The majority of the Blundell Park
crowd that night was made up of
Geordies, many of whom had
travelled to Cleethorpes in the days
before the game to snap up 'home'
tickets. At the whistle, with the First
Division Championship safe,
manager Kevin Keegan was mobbed
by the fans—one of whom placed a
crown upon his head. King Kevin,
indeed.

It was the closest a football match could come to carnival. United signed off from the First Division by slaughtering Leicester City 7–1 at St James' Park on a day of massive emotion which rounded off perfectly everything that had gone before in 1992–93. David Kelly and Andy Cole struck hat-tricks as the capacity crowd basked in everything from sunshine to reflected glory.

Cole, purchased late in the season, took his tally to 12 goals in as many games with the addition of these strikes, while top scorer Kelly took his to 24 for the season. It was the first time in 47 years that two United players had hit three goals in the same match, and Kelly's was the first first-half hat-trick by a Newcastle player in the same 47 years.

United's 1992–93 Championship campaign wasn't built solely on the swashbuckling attacking football for which Keegan's marvellous side became famous. There was a strong, productive midfield and a sturdy defence in which the experience of Barry Venison, signed for £250,000 from Liverpool, was vital. Venison (left of picture) and Steve Howey, destined to become England's centre-half, represented important extra factors in the side.

It is often forgotten in the tumult of the 7–1 romp against Leicester, and the Cole and Kelly hat-tricks, that midfielder Robert Lee scored arguably the best goal of the game. Lee, a regular scorer from midfield, hit the second, working a one-two with Cole on the right then somehow curling an angled shot away from goalkeeper Kevin Poole and inside the far post before wheeling away to celebrate with the Gallowgate End fans.

And so to the Premier League. After a year of riveting, unstoppable football, Tottenham Hotspur provided an altogether different test in the first game of the 1993–94 season. Despite United's best efforts, Spurs put up a solid barrier and pinched victory with a goal on the break from Teddy Sheringham. It was a salutary lesson that life in the top flight would not be so easy.

Defeat at Coventry in the second game meant Keegan's side went to Old Trafford for the third match without a point in their locker, and when Ryan Giggs gave Manchester United the lead the outlook was bleak. But Andy Cole's equaliser removed the doubts and launched United into a long unbeaten run and an eventual third-place finish.

Along the Yellow Brick Road of a memorable season, there were numerous highlights. One came at the end of October 1993, when Wimbledon were despatched 4–0 with Peter Beardsley scoring a hat-trick—the first league goals of his injury-delayed second spell with United. Beardsley's hat-trick included this penalty, rifled confidently past the helpless Hans Segers.

Andy Cole continued on his merry way in the Premier League, scoring eight times in a glorious run of eight league games and extending even that phenomenal rate to 16 in 14. This goal against Wimbledon was the tenth in a sequence which propelled Cole towards a club record 41 in the season.

Amid that amazing run of goals, Cole hit a peak with a first-half hat-trick against Liverpool at St James' Park in mid-November. The Reds had no answer to Cole's predatory instincts, with all three goals scored from single touches around the six-yard line. Liverpool goalkeeper Bruce Grobbelaar was later accused of 'throwing' the game; but Grobbelaar was cleared and the integrity of Cole's achievement remains untainted.

Swindon Town, destined for relegation, never got off the bottom of the table all season and were mere cannon fodder for a rampant United when they came to St James' Park in March 1994. Robert Lee, Steve Watson and Peter Beardsley scored two each in a 7–1 massacre, while Ruel Fox got the other. Remarkably, top scorer Andy Cole failed to find the target in this game.

Beardsley, by now playing at the peak of his powers, scored the first goal from the penalty spot after 12 minutes and Rob Lee added the second six minutes later. It was still 2–0, with 23 minutes to go, when United added five more in 17 minutes, including this, the fourth, from Beardsley on 70 minutes.

The 1993–94 season was a fairytale for everyone at Newcastle United, but for no-one more so than Andy Cole. Cole, ably assisted by 24-goal Peter Beardsley, set a new club record with 41 goals, comprising 34 in the League and seven in the Cups.

No Newcastle player had ever reached 40 goals in a season, but Handy Andy did the trick in the 41st minute of the 40th Premier League match of the season, against Aston Villa at St James' Park. Sent clear by Scott Sellars, Cole rounded Villa 'keeper Nigel Spink and, on the run, fired an angled shot into the open net as he fell. The roar which greeted the goal could have been heard in Timbuktu.

Not satisfied with 40 goals, Andy Cole went one better with a bizarre strike in the final match of the season at home to Arsenal. As the ball spun around in the penalty area, Cole, with his back to goal and lying flat on the pitch, hooked the ball over his head and watched as his effort left keeper Allan Miller helpless.

At the game's end, Arsenal striker Ian Wright, one of Cole's idols, offered his shirt in exchange. For Cole, who started out as a kid at Arsenal, the swap was the icing on the cake of a truly magnificent year.

The terrific achievements of 1993–94 led to qualification for Europe for the first time in 17 years. In the UEFA Cup in 1994–95, United took the bull by the horns, demolishing Royal Antwerp 5–0 in Belgium and 5–2 on Tyneside in the two-legged first round. In Antwerp, Rob Lee created some kind of record with a hat-trick of HEADERS, even barging Andy Cole out of the way to get this one.

Although the European dream was ended by Athletic Bilbao of Spain in the second round, a principal feature of the tie was the friendliness between the two sets of fans. In the northern Spanish town, the fans mixed freely in the streets in great spirits, exchanging colours and drinking together. On the field, the dice fell against United. 3–0 ahead in the first leg at St James', United allowed Bilbao to recover to 3–2, then lost 1–0 to a deflected goal in Bilbao to go out on the away goals rule. Steve Howey's dejection sums up United's exit from Europe.

It seemed in 1994 that Andy Cole would stay at Newcastle longer than Grey's Monument. And when he hit his 68th Newcastle goal in the 1–1 draw with Ipswich Town on November 26th, 1994, nobody could have forecast that it would be his last. But, after nine more goalless games, Cole was sensationally transferred by Kevin Keegan to Manchester United in a £7m part-exchange deal involving Irish winger Keith Gillespie. It was the end of an era—but the doorway to another.

Without Cole for the FA Cup third round replay against Blackburn Rovers at Ewood Park in January 1995, United pulled off a brilliant victory, with Swiss full-back Marc Hottiger opening the scoring early in the second half and Lee Clark grabbing a late winner after Chris Sutton's equaliser for Blackburn. Note the Blackburn player attempting to charge down Hottiger's goalbound shot—his name is Alan Shearer.

Without Cole, United's league form fell away and the side slipped out of a European-qualification place to finish sixth. The FA Cup run ended in the Quarter-Final at Everton. Goals were harder to come by and United won only nine of 21 league games after the turn of the year. One of those victories came on a snowy January night against Wimbledon at St James' Park, when Ruel Fox and stand-in striker Paul Kitson scored the goals in a 2–1 victory.

Kevin Keegan was already planning his rebuilding programme and, unknown to the fans who shivered in the icy conditions that night, one of the players who would join Newcastle was in the Dons side. Right-back Warren Barton, seen here beating Peter Beardsley to the ball, would arrive at Newcastle the following summer for £4m—a then-record price for a British defender.

The indefatigable Beardsley played a major part in keeping United going, finishing 1994–95 as 14-goal second-top scorer—a far cry from the previous season when Beardo was second-top scorer with 24. Although Andy Cole left Newcastle in January, he nevertheless ended top scorer with 15 goals.

Evergreen and ever ready, Beardsley proved a constant danger to defences and here, in the victory over Wimbledon, almost forces home a chance in typically sharp style, only to be denied by the agility of Hans Segers.

Consett-born defender Barry Venison became one of Newcastle United's most dependable assets in the early and middle years of the decade. But while he was as solid as a rock at the back, the one-time skipper was rather less likely to figure at the other end. In 133 games for United he scored just one goal—and this was it, from long range against Aston Villa at St James' Park on February 25th, 1995. Paul Kitson is the first to offer congratulations to the disbelieving scorer.

One of the most exciting matches of the Nineties came along in May 1995: a 3–3 draw against Tottenham Hotspur which contained every imaginable twist and turn. United led 2–0 early on before three Spurs goals in five minutes turned the tables before half-time. In the second half, Peter Beardsley's equaliser earned a point—but that wouldn't have been the case had substitute goalkeeper Mike Hooper, on for the red-carded Pavel Srnicek, not saved Jurgen Klinsmann's penalty with his first touch of the ball.

By the start of the 1995–96 season, Kevin Keegan had recruited three new stars at a cost of £12.5m—and optimism among the fans was renewed. Frenchman David Ginola came to United along with striker Les Ferdinand and defender Warren Barton, and it was Ginola (below), with the film-star looks and mercurial ball skills, who, perhaps, captured the imagination like no other Newcastle player of the era. In the first game of the season, at home to Coventry City, United strolled to a 3–0 victory— but it fell to long-term stalwart Robert Lee (right) to notch the first goal of the campaign.

Newcastle fans have always loved a centre-forward, and £6m Les Ferdinand—quickly dubbed Sir Les—was a No 9 in the grand tradition. Tall and powerful in the air, Ferdinand thrived on the service from the likes of Ginola, and a headed derby winner against Middlesbrough, from a perfect Ginola cross, encapsulated the partnership. Here, Sir Les celebrates in the back of the Middlesbrough net.

In a blistering start to the 1995–96 season, United won nine of their first ten league games, culminating in a bizarre match against Wimbledon at St James' Park. Ferdinand grabbed a hat-trick as Wimbledon lost two defenders through injury before goalkeeper Paul Heald was sent off and the irrepressible Vinnie Jones replaced him in goal. Jones responded to good-natured stick from the fans behind the goal, smilingly strutting around the six-yard box. But Vinnie had to pick the ball out of his net three more times in the 34 minutes he spent between the sticks, as United stormed to a 6–1 win.

One of the most remarkable goals and victories of the decade: close to the end of an epic rearguard battle against Liverpool at Anfield in the fourth round of the Coca-Cola Cup, Steve Watson scores the winner of a lifetime. With injury having deprived United of centre-forward Les Ferdinand, substitute Watson went on a solo run which ended with an exquisite 23-yard chip over the head of Liverpool goalkeeper David James to bring one of the truly great Newcastle United triumphs.

The Coca-Cola Cup run ended in the quarter-finals at Highbury when Arsenal, benefiting from a refereeing decision later admitted to be wrong, kept eleven men on the field to beat ten-man United, without the dismissed David Ginola, 2–0. Les Ferdinand, as always, put his back into it—and needed pain-killing spray from physio Derek Wright to carry on.

In February 1996, with United opening up a 12-point lead at the top of the Premier League, Kevin Keegan spent £7m on Colombian striker Faustino Asprilla. Although Asprilla—nicknamed Tino by the fans—made an immediate impact in a victory at Middlesbrough, many United fans believe to this day that his arrival upset the balance of the side in the run-in, allowing Manchester United to snatch the title at the death.

Asprilla was never very far from trouble, either: in a dramatic 3–3 draw at Manchester City in his third game for the club, he was involved in a violent exchange with City defender Keith Curle which led to lengthy recriminations.

The match—and the defeat—which spelt the beginning of the end for Newcastle United's Championship ambitions came on the first Monday of March 1996, when closest rivals Manchester United, four points behind with a game more played, came to St James' Park and survived a battering to win 1–0 with an Eric Cantona goal. Consequent heartbreaking defeats at Liverpool and Blackburn allowed the Reds to take the title by a four-point margin; but the fact remains that a Newcastle victory on March 4th would have brought the first title since 1927 to Tyneside. The Asprilla–Ferdinand strike partnership failed to pierce the Manchester United defence, and here the Colombian is denied by Denis Irwin.

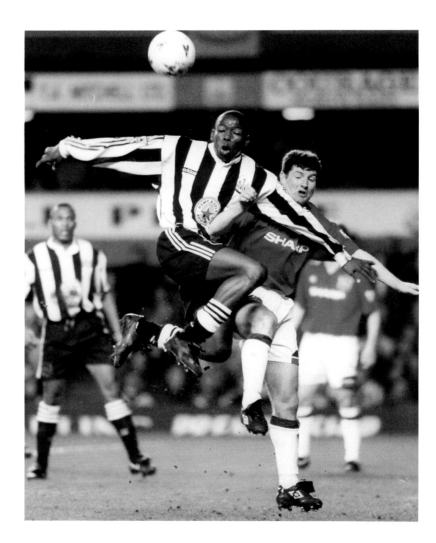

The £15m signing of Blackburn and England striker Alan Shearer in the summer of 1996 would, many believed, be the final piece of Kevin Keegan's Championship jigsaw. But the shadow of Manchester United immediately returned to haunt United and Shearer in the 1996–97 Charity Shield curtain-raiser at Wembley. As if to add insult to injury, the Reds destroyed Newcastle 4–0 and Shearer was, both literally and metaphorically, brought swiftly down to earth.

For Peter Beardsley, like Shearer a Geordie born and bred, the Charity Shield defeat hurt badly. Unlike Shearer, Beardsley had gone through the agony of the previous season's title collapse and was particularly keen to exact revenge.

The fans' army, as always, packed the Tunnel End at Wembley and despite the heartbreak of such a heavy defeat, loyally cheered the players off at the end. Beardsley, as much a fan as a player, returns the applause as he walks, socks down but head up, towards the tunnel.

Alan Shearer's first Newcastle goal wasn't long in coming, and when it came it was well worth waiting for. The £15m Geordie's League debut for United had ended in a disappointing 2–0 defeat at Everton, but four days later, against Wimbledon at St James' Park, the moment came.

United were already ahead 1–0 through an early David Batty goal when they were awarded a free-kick to the left of goal, 25 yards out. Shearer stepped up to curl an impeccable shot around and over the wall and into the far top corner before launching into a goal celebration which was destined to become a more-than-familiar sight in the latter years of the decade.

Back in the UEFA Cup after a one-year absence, United were drawn in the 1996–97 first round against the Swedish amateurs, Halmstads BK. United confirmed their superiority with a superb first-leg performance resulting in a 4–0 victory which rendered the 2–1 second leg defeat in Sweden academic. Tino Asprilla scored the goal of the game at St James' Park with this spectacular flying volley to take the score to 2–0.

The revenge which Newcastle United had long owed Manchester United was finally realised in shattering, spectacular fashion on an October Sunday afternoon in 1996. On an occasion overflowing with thrills and emotion, Kevin Keegan's men ripped the champions to shreds to rattle up a 5–0 victory which will be talked about for very many years to come.

The ball started rolling after 12 minutes when a linesman spotted that Darren Peacock's header had crossed the line before being cleared by Denis Irwin (below).

Further goals followed from David Ginola (30 minutes) Les Ferdinand (63) Alan Shearer (75) and Philippe Albert (83)—the last a sumptuous long-distance chip over goalkeeper Peter Schmeichel.

By now, the Shearer–Ferdinand spearhead was firmly taking effect: after this, the tenth league game of the season, the pair had scored 14 goals between them.

It had seemed the Kevin Keegan dream would never end, but in January 1997 it did—to the consternation of the Geordie Nation. After a drawn FA Cup-tie at Charlton, Keegan quit; the farewell message on the banner at the replay demonstrates the esteem in which he was held.

Former Liverpool and Blackburn manager Kenny Dalglish was appointed as Keegan's replacement 24 hours before the replay against Charlton and, although he did not officially take charge of team affairs until the following match, he couldn't stop himself getting involved in the agonies of life in the dug-out.

Dalglish suffered only two defeats in 16 league games in 1996–97 and by the time of the season's final match, at home to relegated Nottingham Forest, United knew victory would ensure a second-place finish again, but this time, thanks to a change in rules, a place in the Champions League.

On a day when North-East rivals Sunderland and Middlesbrough were both relegated, United swept to a 5–0 victory with Tino Asprilla opening the scoring (below) on 20 minutes and local boy Robbie Elliott rounding it off with the fifth 13 minutes from the end. For Elliott, a Gosforth lad,

it was a remarkable season. Converted from left-back to midfield, he scored four goals in the last seven games, and seven in all to finish United's third-top league scorer behind Alan Shearer (25) and Les Ferdinand (16).

1997–98 became the Alan Shearer Tragedy Story. In a pre-season tournament match against Chelsea at Everton's Goodison Park, Shearer stretched for a last-minute pass and wrecked his right ankle as his studs caught on the rain-soaked surface. The injury was a severe blow to Dalglish's plans, coming as it did just after Les Ferdinand had been sold to Tottenham Hotspur, leaving United without a major strikeforce.

It was six months before Shearer was seen in action again. Following months of arduous recuperation, England's top striker finally bounced back into action as a substitute against Bolton Wanderers at St James' Park on January 17th, 1998. Coming on for John Barnes 18 minutes from time with the score tied at 1–1, Shearer helped launch an all-out assault on the Wanderers goal which brought a 90th-minute winner from Temuri Ketsbaia.

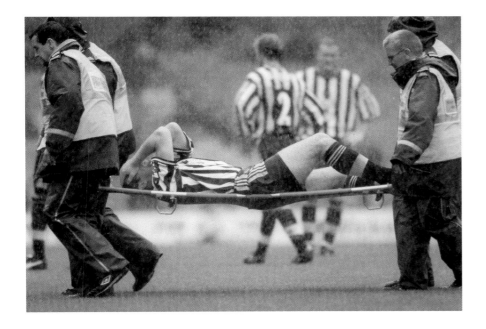

Alan Shearer played twice as substitute before making his first start since his big injury. And when he did line up at the start, it was in the poisoned-chalice FA Cup-tie away to non-league Stevenage Borough. It took just three minutes for Shearer to head in a Keith Gillespie cross—but Stevenage gave United a battle royal, and took the tie to a replay before United eased through 2–1 with two more Shearer goals at St James' Park.

The 1997–98 FA Cup run then took United past Tranmere and Barnsley to the Semi-Final against First Division Sheffield United at Old Trafford, and one of Alan Shearer's greatest moments. With the scoresheet blank and the match finely balanced early in the second half, John Barnes clipped in a cross, Shearer rose to head goalwards and, when keeper Alan Kelly only half-stopped the ball, Shearer pounced like a puma to blast the ball in from almost on the goalline. To 22,000 of his own euphoric people, Shearer raises a triumphant Geordie fist.

The 1998 FA Cup Final proved a very different occasion for Alan Shearer and Newcastle United. Against Arsenal at Wembley, United never performed and were easily beaten, 2–0.

For Shearer, and for his disconsolate team-mates, the nature of the defeat was as disappointing as the defeat itself. Fans who chanted 'attack, attack, attack' blamed manager Dalglish for his over-cautious approach against an Arsenal side destined for the League and Cup double.

Kenny Dalglish parted company with United two games into the 1998–99 season, and the man who replaced him, former Chelsea manager Ruud Gullit, splashed out £8m on Everton striker Duncan Ferguson in late November 1998. Five days later, Ferguson enjoyed a glorious debut, scoring twice in a 3–1 victory over Wimbledon at St James' Park.

There were high hopes that 6ft 4in Ferguson would form a dynamic partnership with Alan Shearer, but a succession of injuries sidelined the giant Scot for long periods.

Manchester United were still the biggest power in England, but the days of Newcastle challenging them for the Premier League title were now past. When the Reds came to Tyneside for the Premier League match of March 1999, they were on their way to their sixth title in eight years, while the Magpies were languishing in mid-table. Peruvian Nol Solano raised hopes of victory with this superb early free-kick, but the champions hit back to win 2–1 with two goals from former Magpie Andy Cole.

Though epic matches were now occurring rather more rarely than in the Keegan years, one such came along at Derby in April 1999. United trailed 1–0 and 2–1, each time equalised within three minutes through Gary Speed, then went into a 4–2 lead through Temuri Ketsbaia and Nol Solano before a late third from Derby. Below, Ketsbaia celebrates his goal with Croatian Silvio Maric, while (right), Rob Lee is denied by the bravery of Derby goalkeeper Russell Hoult.

Old Trafford revisited…a year and six days after the 1998 Semi-Final victory over Sheffield United, Newcastle were back at their 'lucky' ground to face Tottenham Hotspur in the 1999 Semi. Once again, Alan Shearer rose to the occasion, scoring the only two goals of the game in extra time, one a penalty and the second a fulminating 18-yard drive which skidded in off the bar. He even scored them at the same end as in the previous year. The celebration was similar, too—as was the result in the Final, when this time Manchester United won 2–0.

Ruud Gullit's reign, like that of Kenny Dalglish, ended early in the following season. After three defeats and a draw in August 1999, Gullit took United into the home derby against Sunderland with both Alan Shearer and Duncan Ferguson on the bench, and untried youngster Paul Robinson carrying the front-line burden. In a deluge, and with unhappy fans soaked in a half-rebuilt stadium, United sacrificed a 1–0 lead to crash 2–1, and three days later Gullit announced his resignation. Here, in a match many thought should have been abandoned, Gary Speed throws up spray as he challenges Sunderland's Kevin Ball.

Exit Ruud Gullit, enter Bobby Robson. At the age of 66, and after half a century in top-class football at home and abroad, North-Easterner Robson fulfilled a lifelong ambition when he finally took the job he had turned down, out of loyalty to Barcelona, two-and-a-half years before. Robson's first match, at Chelsea, ended in narrow defeat; but his first home game, against Sheffield Wednesday, brought a bewildering 8–0 victory. Robson, an instant crowd favourite, took the cheers of the fans on the pitch before standing back to watch Aaron Hughes head his first goal for Newcastle and set a new high-jump record as well as launching United on the way to their biggest victory since 1946. Alan Shearer scored five of the goals, and Kieron Dyer and Gary Speed one each.

United's European trail in 1999–2000 led through Sofia and Zurich before coming to a halt in the UEFA Cup third round against the Italian giants, AS Roma. Robson, a seasoned European campaigner, had got his tactics absolutely right against CSKA Sofia and FC Zurich, and almost did the trick in 180 momentous minutes against Roma. Only a controversial Francesco Totti penalty in the first leg in Rome separated the sides, but a goalless second leg meant a disappointing exit for United. Here, United's Italian defender Alessandro Pistone takes on Roma defender Antonio Carlos Zago in the Olympic Stadium.

In Newcastle United's dark days, fans used to fantasise about being 3–0 up against one of the world's best teams in the European Cup, with a sensational hat-trick from a mystical striker. All those dreams came true on September 17th, 1997. In their first match in the Champions League, United roared into a 3–0 lead against mighty Barcelona with a hat-trick including a penalty and two headers from the brilliant Tino Asprilla. Barcelona's late fightback left United clinging onto a 3–2 lead in a ferment of excitement around St James' Park. Sadly, the Champions League dream faded and died with a draw and three defeats in the next four group games, but the memory of that night against Barcelona at St James' will never fade.

Warren Barton doesn't often score— and he scores in the last minute even less often. So, when the £4m fullback popped up to score a last-minute winner against Tottenham at St James' Park in October 1997, he was entitled to be just a little ecstatic.

Once again, the FA Cup brought United's best chance of honours in 1999–2000. After beating Tottenham, Sheffield United, Blackburn and Tranmere, Bobby Robson's side was paired with Chelsea in the Semi-Final. Instead of lucky Old Trafford, however, this Semi was played at unlucky Wembley—and unlucky the crumbling national stadium proved again for United. Despite an excellent performance, and a brilliant second-half equaliser from Rob Lee, United were undone by Uruguayan Gustavo Poyet's two goals for Chelsea.

It's ecstasy then agony for Lee, for whom the celebrating hands stretch out after his goal, but upon whom gloom descends after the final whistle.

# The fans

*A Rising Star: For much of two decades until 2000, Newcastle Breweries—originally Scottish & Newcastle—sponsored Newcastle United. Their backing coincided with two periods of great success sparked by Kevin Keegan. The Breweries' blue star overlooks the fans in the Exhibition Stand in a 1995 match against Chelsea.*

*For the first time in 17 years, Newcastle United earned entry into the UEFA Cup in 1994—and blitzed their way past Royal Antwerp of Belgium on a 10–2 aggregate. These two guards at the first leg in Antwerp would have been better employed marking Robert Lee, who scored a brilliant hat-trick of headers in an astonishing 5–0 victory.*

For United's loyal fans, a return to
European competition was the cherry
on an unbelievable cake. A little over
two years earlier, United had
survived relegation to the old
Division Three on the final day of
the 1991–92 season. Then, UEFA
Cup trips to such places as Antwerp
were the stuff of fantasy…in 1994,
the Toon Army made the most of its
fortune.

Octogenarian comedian Sir Norman
Wisdom is an occasional visitor to St
James' Park…and can't resist a bit
of traditional clowning when he gets
there.

Wherever the team goes, the Toon
Army marches with them.

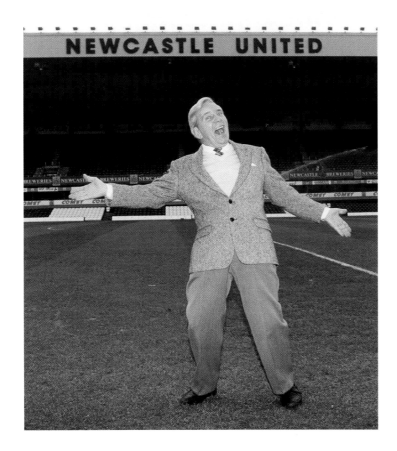

*Prime Minister Tony Blair's Sedgefield constituency is a mere 30 miles to the south of Newcastle, and he too loves to make the occasional trip to St James' Park. Inevitably, the autograph books appear.*

*Army Uniform: A footsoldier of the Toon Army stands cheekily to attention at United's 5–0 Coca-Cola Cup victory away to Bristol City in 1995.*

The 1996 European Championships provided a memorable opportunity for fans of Romania, Bulgaria and France to converge on St James' Park. Designated as Eurofest, the colourful Romanians in particular made the most of it…although the eccentric costumes of four pole-dancers took some imagining and explaining to the bemused Geordies!

After the nightmare of seeing their heroes sacrifice a 12-point lead to finish second behind double champions Manchester United in 1995–96, Newcastle were invited to take part in the Charity Shield curtain-raiser the following August at Wembley…but even with new £15m man Alan Shearer at centre-forward and the Toon Army out in force, Newcastle couldn't avert a 4–0 defeat.

No, these bottles aren't real…but perhaps the mortal Magpie spreadeagled in the shadow of the Twin Towers had a little too much of 'The One And Only'.

Supply and demand: With the ranks of the Toon Army multiplying during the success of the Keegan years, the Adidas sportswear factory in Runcorn, Cheshire, was kept more than busy meeting the demand for the famous black-and-white striped shirt. The backing of Adidas has been a major factor in Newcastle United's rise in the Mighty Nineties.

The David and Goliath FA Cup meeting of United and non-league Stevenage Borough in 1997–98 aroused the interest of the nation. But the very spirit of sport was encapsulated in this photograph of two young and opposing supporters—a picture which adorned the cover of the programme for the replay at St James' Park, which United won 2–1.

The Toon Army's European adventure carried on into the European Champions' Cup in 1997–98, and a qualifying round trip to Croatia Zagreb. The Zagreb fans traditionally link arms over shoulders with backs to the pitch as the pre-match roar intensifies.

The rain in Spain…falls mainly on the Mags. The Champions League trip to Barcelona in November 1997 was supposed to be the pinnacle of every travelling fan's life. But in the event, a rare Spanish downpour dampened the bodies, if not the spirits, of the Toon Army. Exposed to the elements on the high terraces of a near-deserted Nou Camp, the Geordies loyally backed their team through a disappointing performance in a 1–0 defeat.

The 1997 UEFA Cup quarter-final trip to Monaco meant an opportunity for the United fans to sample the millionaire lifestyle on France's south coast. But the Monagesque police were as mean as Monaco, who won 1–0 at St James' and 3–0 in the Principality.

Black-and-white support: For one female fan, the word strip is taken a little too literally.

A 4–0 UEFA Cup first round home leg victory over Swedish amateurs Halmstads in 1996 rendered the return leg academic. But the Toon Army was there as always…to begin a tour which would take them to Budapest, Metz and Monaco.

Howay the lad: Geordie actor Robson Green makes no secret of his love for the Magpies, and travels to matches from his North-East home whenever commitments allow.

The 1994 UEFA Cup trip to Bilbao in northern Spain remains one of the greatest memories of all for the travelling Newcastle supporters in the 1990s. Spaniards and Geordies caroused, drank and sang together in the streets of the Spanish city and many friendships were formed. Even a 1–0 defeat to Bilbao, and an away-goals exit from Europe, could not dim the warmth of the memories.

The welcome was no less warm inside the San Mames Stadium in Bilbao. Spanish fans clamoured for the autograph of United boss Kevin Keegan before the match and Keegan, as ever, was happy to oblige.

*Not many travelling fans would call Old Trafford their lucky ground, but for Newcastle's loyal supporters the home of Manchester United means joy unconfined. In 1998, the Geordies took over the stadium to hail the 1–0 FA Cup Semi-Final defeat of Sheffield United with a goal from Alan Shearer.*

*Wherever you go, you're sure to find a Geordie, goes the song. And these three from Winlaton make their presence known in Zurich.*

The second successive FA Cup Semi-Final trip to Old Trafford came in 1999 when, under Ruud Gullit, United took on and conquered Tottenham Hotspur with two extra-time goals from the previous season's hero, Alan Shearer. The head of Gullit goes up close to pitchside… and as for the other fan with the Breweries' blue star logo shaved on—well, they do say Brown Ale goes to your head.

*They come in all drapes and guises
…United fans at the 1999 FA Cup
Semi-Final against Spurs.*

When United returfed the St James' Park pitch in 1996, the club offered sections of it for sale to supporters. Christopher Scott, 11, of Wallsend, buys up his piece of the hallowed turf.

The end of an era: in January 1997 Kevin Keegan, hero and idol of all Tyneside, stunned the football world by quitting as manager of Newcastle United. As the news spread, thousands of extra copies of the Newcastle Evening Chronicle were sold on the streets—and to fans like these who gathered outside St James' Park, scarcely able to believe the news.

Jackie Milburn was a United hero of the '50s, and the statue of him outside St James' Park's south-west corner proved a magnet in the very different '90s.

Champions we aren't: one young fan had the word 'Champions' sewn onto her woollen doll's foot as Newcastle opened up a 12-point Premiership lead over Manchester United in 1996. But, at the season's end, the Red Devils had snatched the title.

The late Cardinal Basil Hume was an ardent fan of Newcastle United, and on a visit to St James' Park in 1997 shares a joke with United Chief Executive Freddie Fletcher.

Racing tipster John McCririck never misses a chance to demonstrate his love for Newcastle United and at the 1998 FA Cup Final he turned up in his finest regalia.

*The bottom line: United's Champions League trip to Barcelona in 1997 was memorable for everything but the match—a 1–0 wash-out in torrential storms at a deserted stadium. But these two cheeky Geordie lasses made their loyalties clear in the city centre before the match.*

*If the hat fits…a quartet of Geordie fans don traditional Spanish sombreros on their way to the Nou Camp.*

*(overleaf)*
*Nice to have Metz you: illuminated by the light of flares, fans of French club Metz create a thrilling atmosphere at the UEFA Cup third round clash with Newcastle in the Stade Saint-Symphorien on November 19th, 1997. A Peter Beardsley penalty put out the French lights in a 1–1 draw, and two Tino Asprilla goals won the return leg at St James' Park.*

# The officials & The board

NEWCASTLE UNITED

In the late '80s, with Newcastle United struggling on and off the field, and with St James' Park half-built, the rebel Magpie Group launched a power bid that would change the face of the club forever. Led by millionaire MetroCentre developer John Hall, the consortium pledged a better, brighter future for United. At a Magpie Group Press conference, John Hall (standing)—not yet a Sir—is flanked by (left to right): Malcolm Dix, David Stephenson, Brian Reed and Joe Robertson.

Newcastle United Chairman Gordon McKeag responded to the Magpie Group's high-finance take-over bid—their offer of £1,000 per share in 1988 tempted many to sell—by pleading with shareholders to remain loyal. But McKeag was fighting against the tide.

As a public orator, Hall had few peers—and when he took the show on the road, United fans flocked to hear him outline a new future. Here, Hall comes face-to-face with the fans for the first time as he addresses a 500-strong gathering of the United Supporters For Change faction at High Pit Social Club in Cramlington, Northumberland.

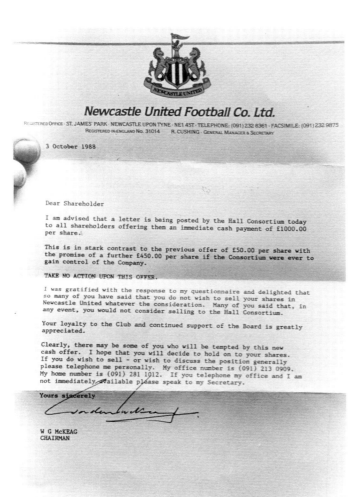

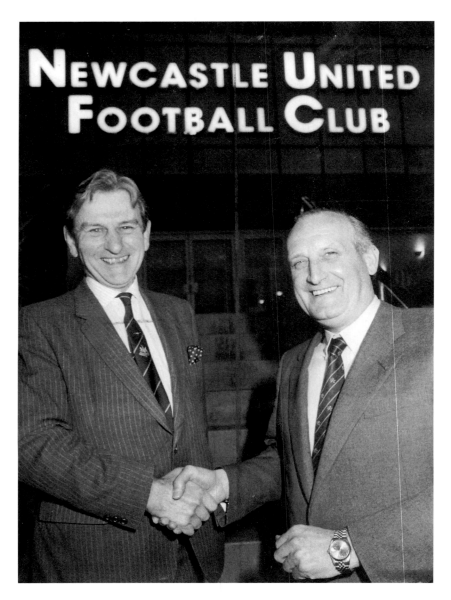

In 1990, McKeag (left) held out an olive branch to Hall by inviting the Magpie Group leader to join the Board of Directors at Newcastle United. It was, apparently, a solution to a dispute which had torn the club apart and had, unhappily, coincided with relegation from the First Division in 1989. Hall accepted the invitation after two sessions of talks and symbolically shook hands with his former opponent on the St James' Park steps.

Hall (third from left) takes his place in the Boardroom in 1990, and takes his first steps towards the better future the Magpie Group had promised. Alongside Hall are (left to right): Bob Young, Peter Mallinger, Stan Seymour, George Forbes, Gordon McKeag and Russell Cushing. Only Cushing—now Director of Football Administration, company secretary for the football club and, from July 18th, plc secretary—is directly involved today in the day-to-day running of United. Young is now Honorary President.

In February '92, Ossie Ardiles was sacked and Kevin Keegan brought in to take his place. It was a bold gamble—and one which paid off. United survived, and within months, boosted by the rush of enthusiasm the Keegan signing had generated among the fans, Sir John took complete control of the club. There was still work to do, but from the start of 1992–93 there would be no looking back.

On a tidal wave of emotion, United swept aside all opposition in the 1992–93 First Division season, winning 11 successive League games at the outset and finishing eight points clear to take the Championship. Before the final match of the season Sir John went onto the pitch to acknowledge the fans, then watched in glee as United turned on the style as never before to swamp Leicester City 7–1 —a match which has since taken on an almost mythical quality in the memories of the supporters.

The Strawberry pub just off the south-east corner of St James' became a regular meeting-place for a wealthy Chairman, who never lost the common touch, and the supporters who backed his dream all the way. After the First Division Championship win of 1993, Sir John again returned to The Strawberry to celebrate with the fans.

For all that promotion had achieved, much work had still to be done on the stadium and a new development plan was drawn up. On the terraces which would soon disappear, Sir John, Chief Executive Freddie Fletcher (left), who had joined Newcastle United in January 1992, and then-general manager Russell Cushing display the plans.

*The rise and rise of Newcastle United had been fast in the extreme and Sir John continued to operate in the fast lane with the development of the Lister Storm racing car in 1996. The car was raced abroad…but never matched the success of the football club whose name was emblazoned on the front.*

*Behind every great man there's a great woman—and Lady Mae, wife of Sir John Hall, quietly and proudly supported her husband during his era of achievement at Newcastle United.*

*Club Patron Trevor Bennett was one of the club's most important benefactors in the early '90s, and travels from his Midlands home to watch the team. Here, he compares notes with coach Arthur Cox.*

The Newcastle United directors had plenty to cheer about in the Nineties—but rarely more so than in Zagreb on a memorable August night in 1997. A dramatic Temuri Ketsbaia goal in the final minute of extra time in the qualifier against Croatia Zagreb had assured United of a golden passage into the money-spinning Champions League, and the top brass show off their feelings in no uncertain terms.

The treatment room is normally an inner sanctum, but, in February 1995, United fan Paul Henderson won a 'Day in the Life' competition and was allowed behind the scenes at the training ground. Paul joins Derek Wright in taking a look at Belgian international Philippe Albert.

United's long-serving physiotherapist Derek Wright is one of the most respected medical men in the game and since joining United in 1984 has seen and treated every injury known to footballers. Here he treats England striker Les Ferdinand's right foot problem in 1995.

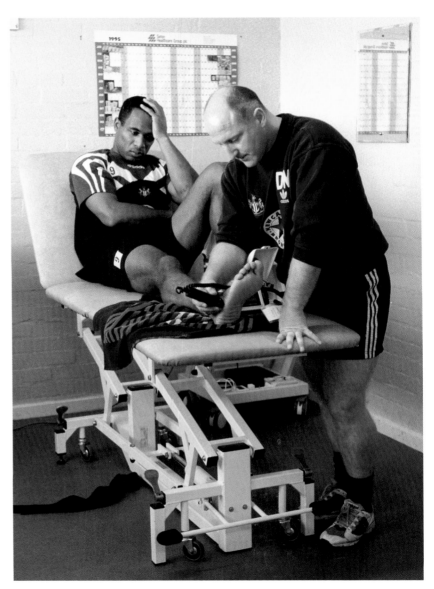

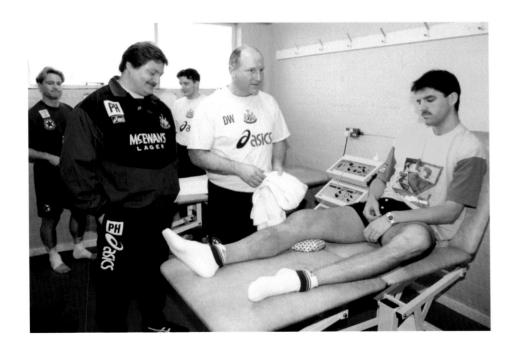

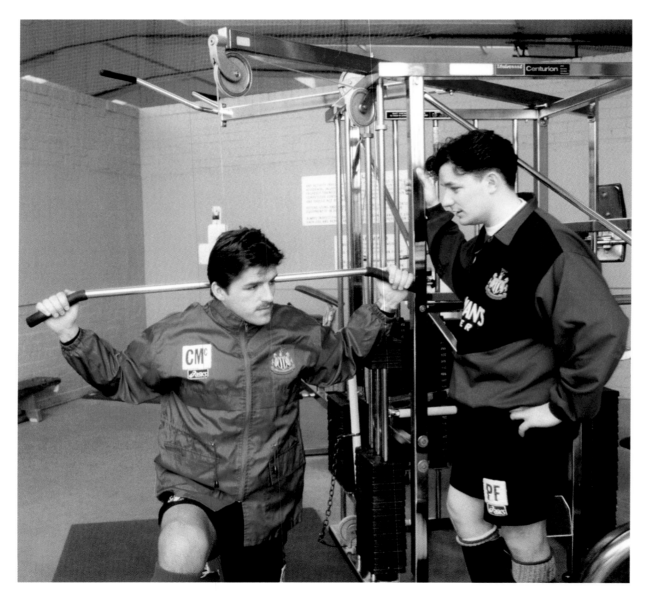

*Wright's sidekick Paul Ferris, once United's youngest-ever debutant in 1982, rejoined the club as a physio in 1993 and plays a vital role in the ever-busy treatment room. Here, he supervises Philippe Albert's weight training.*

*...and together, they make a great team. Ferris and Wright together.*

*Together again: In 1983–84, Arthur Cox managed United to promotion with Kevin Keegan his team captain and Terry McDermott a driving force in midfield. Ten years later, the triumvirate was together again, this time with Keegan manager, McDermott assistant manager, and Cox coach. With the exception of Keegan, even the haircuts were the same!*

*Alan Shearer's devastating ankle injury in 1997 gave Wright and Ferris one of their most demanding and detailed recovery missions. It was six months before the England centre-forward could play again, and in that time Shearer went through numerous special exercises—including, under Wright's watchful eye, special swimming pool exercises to build up his muscles.*

*You HAVE got a prayer, son! United Club Chaplain Reverend David Tully chats with midfield star Scott Sellars at the Durham training ground. The Chaplain is always on hand to give the players advice and guidance on their private lives.*

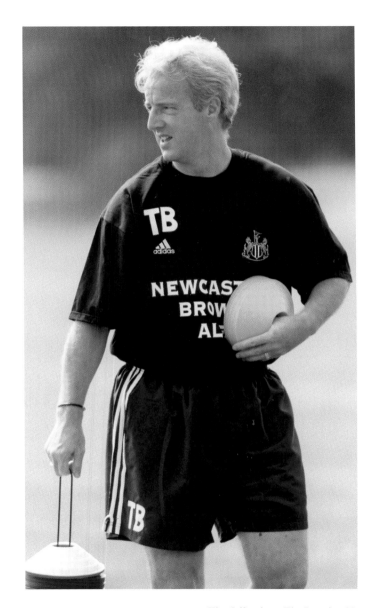

They called Terry McDermott 'The Buffer' for taking the pressure off bosses Kevin Keegan and Kenny Dalglish. McDermott played for Newcastle in the '70s then his home-town club Liverpool (with both Keegan and Dalglish) before returning to United with Keegan for the 1982–1984 promotion push, and the Mighty Nineties.

Former Celtic manager Tommy Burns joined another ex-Celtic idol, Kenny Dalglish, as a coach at Newcastle in 1997. But, anxious to pursue his career as a manager, he left to join Reading the following year.

*What a line-up: but this impressive rack of high-profile team shirts behind kit man Ray Thompson is only for Peter Beardsley and the guest players at his testimonial in January 1999.*

*One of United's hard-working backroom boys, kit man Ray Thompson, doubles as a drinks waiter for the players working up a thirst on the training ground.*

*Need your lawn cut? Groundsman George Green gets ready to take a bit off the top of the hallowed turf.*

*The end of an era: It is December 1997, and Sir John Hall, after five years as Chairman of Newcastle United, announces with a wistful look in his eyes that he is stepping down.*

*Sir John's replacement, Freddy Shepherd, made a special presentation 'from all at Newcastle United Football Club'. And the debt of gratitude was vast.*

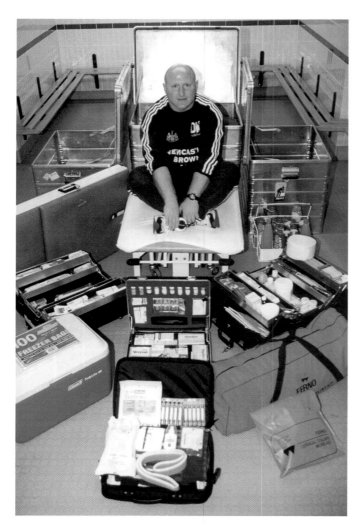

Prepared: the well-equipped physio has a massive array of everything imaginable for the footballing injury victim. It's a far cry from the old days of the magic sponge and a bucket of water.

The Tartan Terror: United's Glaswegian Reserve Team coach Tommy Craig warms up for the Euro 2000 Scotland–England clash by donning tam o'shanter, Braveheart orange wig, and Scotland banner. But Craig's English colleagues had the last laugh.

When United qualified for the 1997–98 Champions League, the face of the stadium changed for all three home matches. The UEFA spotted matchball symbol was pasted across the advertising boards—the first few are visible at the back of the East Stand as Operations Manager Paul Stevens organises the UEFA Champions League work crew.

Former Liverpool defender Mark Lawrenson was brought to United by Kevin Keegan as a defensive coach in 1996…and picked up some early advice from that arch-destroyer of defences, Colombian international striker Tino Asprilla.

Fitness programmes can take you anywhere—even up a mountain in the Lake District. United centre-back Steve Howey was taken trekking up the 2,288ft Pavey Ark and 2,403ft Harrrison Stickle, between Coniston and Windermere, by physio Derek Wright and masseur Mick Greener (standing) to help strengthen his leg several months after rupturing an Achilles tendon.

*Newcastle United's longest-serving administrative official, Russell Cushing, overlooks St James' Park. Cushing, now Director of Football Administration, company secretary of the football club, and plc secretary, has three decades of service with United.*

No man worked harder than Chief
Executive Freddie Fletcher to raise
the financial profile of Newcastle
United Football Club and pull off
the Nineties miracle. A tough-
talking Scot, formerly with Glasgow
Rangers, Fletcher revitalised a club
with debts of £6m to help turn it into
a multi-million-pound empire. His
methods may not always have been
popular, but Newcastle United
would not have been in such a strong
position today without his influence.

*Former Leeds, Arsenal and Middlesbrough centre-forward Ray Hankin—a Wallsend-born Geordie—runs United's successful Football in the Community programme. Normally, Ray coaches the youngsters on the pitch, but in 1999–2000 he took time out to help a band of children devise a Tune for the Toon.*

# The New Castle

NEWCASTLE UNITED

The way we were…at the start of the Nineties, St James' Park was a sorry sight: half-built, wide open to the elements, and desperately in need of a financial injection.

The Milburn Stand to the left, built at crippling cost shortly before the relegation of 1989, sat uncomfortably opposite the East Stand of 1973 and alongside north, south and west terraces which had stood since 1905 but which were to be condemned in the Taylor Report which followed the Hillsborough disaster of 1989. The one-time pride of St James', the Leazes End terrace at the top of the picture, was but a sad fragment of former days. The antiquated Gallowgate End, nearest the camera, had little going for it and facilities which belonged in the Stone Age.

St James' Park needed a miracle. And it got it.

With the demands of the Taylor Report pressing ever harder, United had to move quickly to complete stadium work. In January 1994, as demolition of the rear Gallowgate End terrace began, the fans were condensed into the front half and brought into the ground via a side gate, walking along the cinder track and clambering over the advertising hoardings to take their places.

By 1994, after the Sir John Hall Stand at the Leazes (north) End was built, the Exhibition (south) Stand was beginning to take shape. The pace of the development was rapid, but the old west and south terraces were still in place, and St James' Park would not become an all-seater stadium until the summer of 1995. Is Chairman Sir John Hall hailing the old…or the new?

*In 1995, the final corner sections were filled in and covered to have the new stadium complete and ready for the start of the 1995–96 season. The South-West corner was designed to house new offices and the exclusive Magpie Room restaurant—the only football stadium restaurant to appear in a Good Food Guide.*

From outside the Newcastle
Breweries building, the scale of the
South (Exhibition) Stand and new
South-West corner section is clear.
The Milburn (West) Stand to the
left would within five years be raised
even higher to more than match the
height of the Gallowgate End South
Stand.

High up in the South-West corner, a
welder fixes into place a metal safety
barrier on what was then one of the
highest points in the stadium.

The old metal gates bearing the Newcastle United Football Club crest are closed at the Gallowgate End entrance as the South-West corner takes shape, rising to the height of the South Stand on the right.

The man who masterminded the rebuilding of St James' Park, Russell Jones, deserves massive credit for its glorious appearance today, but he remains essentially the quiet man of the Newcastle United Board. Jones, who worked for Sir John Hall at Cameron Hall Developments, was handed the task of devising the best possible future for Newcastle United's home, and when alternative schemes to build a new stadium elsewhere ran into insurmountable planning difficulties, he worked miracles to extend the landlocked St James' to the new Millennium capacity of 52,000.

In the summer of 1995, St James' Park was to all intents and purposes complete. But the 36,000 capacity was never enough for a club of Newcastle United's magnitude, and with sell-outs at virtually every home match, the rebuilding would soon resume.

In early 1995, the two ends of St James' Park provide a striking contrast. Looking from the South Stand (left picture), the North Stand opposite curves and blends smoothly into the West and East Stand structures.

But from the North Stand, the South Stand opposite rises separate from the two touchline stands, with no corner sections yet in place. However, by the start of the 1995–96 season, the full circle was complete.

For many a long year, the Gallowgate End was the poorest part of St James' Park—an open terrace, exposed to the elements, and with rather primitive facilities, it was the least expensive section of the ground from which to watch. But the ambitions of United's new Board changed all that, and in 1994 the proud new Exhibition Stand banished the old ghosts and memories.

Engineers who test-drilled the ground before rebuilding found underground weaknesses caused by old mine workings, and had to strengthen the foundations of the new stand.

From down below—two workmen
are dwarfed by the massive new
South Stand.

From up above—the South Stand is
in its turn dwarfed by the gigantic
construction crane behind.

From a vantage point on top of the
new Exhibition Stand roof, its height
is made vividly clear. To the left and
right the West and East Stands
appear minuscule by comparison;
the wooded expanse of Leazes Park
beyond the North Stand also comes
into view.

In the main car park fronting onto Barrack Road, the old administrative block is finally swept away by the bulldozers. In the 1960s, the building was used as an indoor gymnasium for the players to train in during bad weather. In later years it housed the Development Association office and club shop, then was converted into offices above with the multi-windowed ticket office below.

When the Milburn Stand replaced the old wooden West Stand in 1988, the vaulted roof was considered one of the most modern structures of its time. But, overtaken by progress, the horizontal concrete roof supports are gradually demolished in 2000 to make way for the upper tier of the Milburn Stand. A 'nibbler' demolition vehicle is used to 'eat' its way through the remains of the old roof.

Around 60 metres above ground level, a workman looks down on St James' Park from the safety platform.

The transparent cantilever roof cover which makes the Milburn Stand one of the lightest and airiest in the country is put into place by workmen on a series of sliding platforms, while seats are installed in the upper tier.

St James' Park nears its full majesty, with the Milburn Stand adding a new dimension to the city skyline. Two massive cranes dominate the magnificent new structure—and completion is now just months away.